MW01143056

Aru

in the Solomon Islands

Text and photographs by Alain Chenevière

Translated by Lisa Davidson

Lerner Publications Company
Minneapolis

All words that appear in **bold** are explained in a glossary on page 58.

This edition first published in the United States in 1996 by Lerner Publications Company, 241 First Avenue North, Minneapolis, Minnesota 55401.

© Hachette Livre 1994. Originally produced as *Aru: L'enfant sorcier* in 1994 by Hachette Livre, Paris, France. Text and photographs by Alain Chenevière.

Library of Congress Cataloging-in-Publications Data

Chenevière, Alain.
    [Aru, l'enfant sorcier. English]
    Aru in the Solomon Islands / by Alain Chenevière : translated by Lisa Davidson.
        p. cm. — (My future)
    Includes index.
    Summary: Text and photographs present the story of twelve-year-old Aru, the son of a medicine man in a village in the Solomon Islands.
    ISBN 0–8225–2827–4 (lib. bdg.)
    1. Malaita (Solomon Islands)—Social life and customs—Juvenile literature. 2. Shamans—Solomon Islands—Malaita—Juvenile literature. 3. Children—Solomon Islands—Malaita—Juvenile literature. 4. Solomon Islands—Juvenile literature.
[1. Solomon Islands—Social life and customs.] I. Title.
II. Series.
DU850.C4413 1996
995.93'7—dc20   95–31073
                                                                       CIP
                                                                        AC

Printed in France by I.M.E.
Bound in the United States of America
1 2 3 4 5 6 — 01 00 99 98 97 96

Contents

The island of Malaita lies to the east of Australia in the Pacific Ocean. Just a tiny speck on the map, the island is part of an **archipelago** called the Solomon Islands. Malaita is the longest island in the archipelago. The islanders say Malaita is shaped like a sleeping dog.

Malaita is the most mysterious and untamed of all the Solomon Islands. In the damp heat, the sweetish smell of mildew rises from the thick green forest. This steamy jungle is home to many multicolored birds.

Among the tribes that live on Malaita, some—it is said—are still headhunters. But this is no longer true of the Kwara'ae people. This tribe, one of the largest on Malaita, lives on the western coast of the island and on the small, artificial island of Laulasi that lies just off the western shore.

Laulasi is also the name of the village on the artificial island where Aru Maelaua lives. With all its huts huddled up against one another, Laulasi looks like a fairy-tale village. At first glance, visitors might think they're imagining what they are seeing. Kwara'ae children, playing a game similar to hopscotch, have dark skin and very light—almost white—hair.

Aru Maelaua is one of them. Like his younger brother Wilson, Aru has magnificent blond hair that falls in golden curls on his shoulders. Standing in front of their home, the two brothers were arguing.

"I haven't been able to find my brown sack ever since you went through the whole house," declared Aru. "What did you do with my sack?"

Twelve-year-old Aru crossed his arms over his chest and glared at his brother. Wilson tried to deny everything.

"But I didn't touch anything, I swear!"

"Don't swear. I know what you did," declared Aru. "Last week you gathered a bunch of shells from the beach and hid them in the house. I remember, I was here. You even asked me to leave while you hid them."

"That's true . . . " sighed Wilson.

"And then, because you're so absentminded, you forgot where you put the shells. And ever since, you've been frantically looking every-where. And what happened? Everything is turned all upside down. You'll see what Papa says when he gets home!"

"I didn't touch Papa's plants!" Ambu, their father, was the **medicine man** of the village. His herbs and flowering plants were used for healing.

"But you did touch mine," continued Aru, not letting up. "You mixed up all the plants I had put out to dry, and I can't find my magic sack anywhere. So go on, admit it."

"Okay, it's true, I moved your things around a little bit," admitted Wilson, lowering his head. "But I put everything back the way I found it. It's not all that messed up."

"What you did was very bad," interrupted Aru. "You shouldn't touch Papa's magic or mine. You know I have to go before the Council of

Elders in a month, Wilson, and all you do is mess up my work."

"I won't do it anymore, I promise. If you like, I'll help you clean up . . . "

But Aru turned on his heels, and ignoring Wilson's offer, went into the house to look for his sack.

Wilson understood why his brother had gotten so angry. He knew Aru had an important role to play in the village. In fact, Wilson was pleased that his very own brother had been chosen to follow their father as the village medicine man.

Two years ago, Aru had started on the path of "Great Knowledge." Patiently, he learned about the plants used in the magic recipes. His father taught Aru the secrets of the art of healing. And now, in less than one month, Aru would have to go through the final tests of his initiation—in the presence of the Council of Elders and the Shark Priest. Although Wilson didn't like being scolded by his older brother, he was certainly proud of Aru!

Exactly 26 days later, Aru stood before the Council of Elders, who had gathered in David Wairamu's hut. The face of David Wairamu—the great Shark Priest—was wrinkled but somehow appeared ageless. He had not uttered a single word or made the slightest movement since the beginning of the ceremony.

The priest was surrounded by the three oldest chiefs of the clan. They had arrived for the occasion from Talakali, a large Kwara'ae village on the coast of Malaita. Aru felt very small among all these important people. Fortunately, the boy's father stood at his side. Ambu's presence alone reassured the boy tremendously.

Long ago, Aru's mother had died during a **dysentery** epidemic. Aru was only four years old at the time of his mother's death, while Wilson was still just a baby. Neither of the boys had any strong memories of their mother. They had learned everything they knew from their father, who had never remarried and was bringing up his sons alone. Aru had grown very close to his father.

A deep silence reigned in the hut. Outside, night was falling. The village barely stood out against the dark mass of forest. A few muted cries sounded from among the trees—the nocturnal animals were preparing for the hunt. This evening, like every evening, a fine rain fell until dusk. Flickering lights soon appeared in the huts.

Aru shivered. As part of his initiation, the Elders had asked the boy to prepare a potion to fight swamp fever. He patiently performed the same gestures his father had taught him, sorting the ingredients from his sack and murmuring the magic words. Everything seemed to be going well. Then suddenly, Aru forgot everything, right in the middle of his test.

Two red seeds, one green. His hands hesitated—he no longer knew which seed to take. He had carefully sorted the bones, herbs, and seeds, figured out the different combinations, and repeated the sacred formulas he had learned for more than a year, but somehow now his mind had gone blank. Would he now fail, when he was so close to reaching his goal?

With motionless, piercing eyes, the Elders watched him. They saw every movement, every hesitation. Desperate, Aru looked to his father for comfort. Ambu's laughing eyes and peaceful smile showed Aru how much his father believed in him. It meant a lot to the young boy. Suddenly he noticed that his father had moved his left arm slightly. Was it a message? On Ambu's wrist hung a bracelet of reddish stones. The red stones!

In a flash, the child understood the message. With calm confidence, Aru picked up the two red seeds and placed them on the pile of herbs he had already sorted. The gray seed went on the pile to the right. Everything came back to him now, and the test seemed easy. In a few minutes, he had finished the task the Elders had asked him to perform. Seven small piles were lined up in front of him. He checked them once more, just for form—he knew he had already passed this test. Then, with a profound weight off his shoulders, he raised his head to look directly at the silent, waiting adults.

One by one, they all leaned over the small piles. The last to look was the old Wairamu, who counted and recounted the number of seeds and leaves with his bony fingers. Each time he finished checking he let out a "Wah" of satisfaction, which was immediately repeated by the other men.

"Wah!" Wairamu had reached the seventh pile. The hut resounded with the cry, and Aru's heart beat so hard he thought it would burst. The priest looked straight into the boy's eyes and, after an unbearable silence, let fall two words from his thin lips.

"It's good."

Aru was overjoyed, but he didn't show it—that would not be appropriate. He merely looked at his father out of the corner of his eyes and thought, "thank you, Papa."

One by one, the clan leaders gave their opinions.

"You will be a great medicine man, Aru," declared the first.

"People will come from far away to see you," continued the second.

"Honor will come to your village and to all of the Kwara'ae," added the third.

The boy could not have been happier, and his heart overflowed with joy. He had succeeded! The path of the Great Knowledge was now open to him!

The test was over, and no one paid Aru any further attention. The Elders had started up what would be a long conversation. Aru took advantage of the moment to slip out of the hut into the soft night. A countless number of stars shone in the sky, and a sweet perfume reached him from the forest.

The sleeping village looked so beautiful to Aru that he finally dared to express the joy that overwhelmed him. First quietly, then increasingly louder, his joyous cry rose up above the houses, passed over the top of the trees, and disappeared into the forest.

It had been raining non-stop for three days. The ground had been transformed into a mud pit, and a thick fog floated over the village. The pale light of the sun barely shone through the mist. Tired of waiting for the weather to clear, Aru took his canoe in the morning and paddled across to the coast of Malaita, where he entered the thick forest to collect the leaves that his father needed for medicines.

Aru had been walking for about two hours and his sack was almost half full. At mid-morning, the rain finally stopped, only to be replaced by a suffocating heat that increased as the clouds cleared. The boy was sweating heavily, and all around him the forest seemed to be doing the same—channels of warm water dripped from the leaves of the green and purple liana vines that wrapped around the tree trunks.

Suddenly, Aru noticed he had stepped into a slimy swamp. The warm water rose up to his heels. Yech! Leeches attached themselves to his legs, and mosquitoes began biting him. Aru batted his arms wildly, though unsuccessfully, to chase the bugs away. He decided to return home. "I've collected enough leaves. I'm going back to the village," he muttered to himself in the quiet of the swamp.

But just at that moment, he heard a sharp snapping sound, then two more. The noises had come from his right. Then Aru heard whispering. As fast as lightning, the boy crouched down behind a tree. He grabbed handfuls of mud, which he smeared over his hair, his face, and his body. He then lay down in the stagnant water and pulled a few leaves over him. It was the best way to go unnoticed.

Aru had been told and retold—encounters in the forest were rarely friendly. Since the early days of his childhood, the boy had heard stories that made him shudder. Murders, kidnappings, and other mysterious events . . . he shivered just thinking about this.

The sounds came closer, but slowly—too slowly. Each moment that passed seemed like an hour to Aru. Suddenly, the leaves opened just a few paces in front of him. A hand appeared, then another, holding a long spear. A man's fierce face then loomed up, his forehead encircled with a string of human teeth. His body appeared, followed by another man, then a third.

Burrowed in the slimy water of the swamp, Aru's heart beat wildly, and he could hear his own pulse hammering in his veins. He recognized the large clubs and sharpened spears of the Kwaio, the ferocious warriors from the mountains, feared by all the inhabitants of Malaita. No one had ever been able to conquer the Kwaio, not even the British soldiers who carried big guns and other fancy weapons.

Young Aru was overcome by an uncontrollable shaking. He placed his hand over his mouth to stifle the scream of terror that was rising from his chest. Four more Kwaio warriors loomed out of the dark jungle, armed and intimidating. There were seven of them altogether. Aru didn't dare even raise his eyes, fearing the Kwaio would feel his glance. "But no," he silently repeated to reassure himself, "I am well hidden. They will pass by without seeing me."

A sudden hush fell over the swamp. What was happening? Where were the Kwaio? Aru raised his head carefully and looked in front of him. Oh no! With a shock he saw his medicine bag, which he had dropped in haste, lying on the ground not far from the Kwaio.

The first warrior saw it and quickly gestured to the others. One of them lifted up the sack, smelled it, and showed it to the other warriors. Instantly, all seven Kwaio bent over on the defensive, holding their weapons aloft and rolling their fearsome eyes. The men looked like wild animals on the trail of their prey, as they began to search the area for the owner of the bag.

Aru was overcome with panic. They would no doubt find him—it was just a matter of minutes. Some of the Kwaio were still headhunters—they would cut Aru into pieces and maybe even eat him. The boy was paralyzed by his deep-seated fear. His throat felt so dry that he could not breathe. He could almost feel the blow of a club that would smash his skull.

One of the Kwaio came near Aru's hiding place. The warrior stood so close that Aru could have reached out to touch the man's feet. Another step and the man would walk right on top of Aru. Frozen with terror, the boy watched the bare feet of the warrior edge closer.

Then a miracle occurred. Just as the warrior was about to discover the boy, a sudden movement rustled the branches of a nearby tree. A large, brightly colored bird flew out from the leaves.

A coucal! The seven men instantly abandoned their search and began to chase the bird. Aru could hear the guttural cries of the warriors on the hunt. Coucal feathers were highly prized. Catching this prey was more important than finding the owner of the sack.

Aru waited a moment to be sure that the Kwaio were out of range, then panting, he sat up in the mud and started to cry. He thought his last moments on earth had come. While the tears flowed, he again spotted the coucal flying overhead. Without the help of the bird, he probably would already be dead.

A sudden thought occurred to Aru. According to Kwara'ae legend, the coucal was linked to the shark, whose spirit protected all members of the tribe. "Did the shark send the bird to save me, a mere initiate?" wondered Aru with a shiver of awe mixed with joy and pride. This idea reassured him so much that he stopped crying.

The aqua sea shimmered against the blue sky. Aru stood perfectly motionless in water up to his waist. In the calm of the lagoon, an enormous shark swam around him as regularly as clockwork. Three circles, then four. The shark was closing in. Aru did not move a muscle.

The boy held a slab of raw meat in his outstretched hands. The previous night, a pig had been sacrificed so that the young initiate could offer the animal's flesh to the shark-god. It was an important step in the path of the Great Knowledge. Aru realized this. For days he had been preparing for this moment in secret ceremonies. His self-confidence explained his calmness as he faced the enormous gray shape that moved toward him.

Last evening and this morning, David Wairamu, even more solemn than usual, gave Aru a bitter, brownish potion to drink. The liquid melted away the boy's fear and gave him a great feeling of inner calm. Yet, despite everything he had been told, Aru knew that accidents sometimes happened. He wouldn't weigh much between the fearsome jaws of the shark.

Suddenly, the side of the shark rose up right beside Aru. A black, expressionless eye peered at the boy for a brief moment, and then the shark once again dove beneath the surface, brushing against Aru's legs. The beast came up again, stopping abruptly, and waited motionless under the water's surface. Aru could have touched the huge animal, but he had been told not to do anything that could frighten the shark-god.

His outstretched arms trembled with fatigue. A drop of blood oozed from the raw meat and fell into the water. It was the signal! The large pointed snout of the shark rose up in front of Aru, who couldn't stop himself from jerking back.

Too late! The pink and white jaws opened wide, revealing three rows of jagged teeth, and lunged forward to grab the meat. A brutal blow shook the boy's left arm, and he heard a dull crunch and a sudden sucking noise.

"My hand! It ripped my hand off!" he screamed.

But his hand was still there. He looked wide-eyed at his empty hand. The shark had disappeared, leaving not the slightest scratch on the young initiate. The shark had taken the offering held in the boy's hands and had left him unharmed. "So the legend is right," thought Aru, his heart full of relief and joy. The shark-god will not attack the initiates of Malaita.

Behind him, on shore, stood his family and the entire village, watching. They had seen the shark-god accept the sacred offering and swim out into the open sea. Ambu, standing in front of the group, beamed with pride. He knew the shark-god had accepted his son.

"Do you know why Joseph has hairy, buck-led legs?" asked small Tamu mischievously.

The five boys burst out laughing. Aru turned around to see Joseph's reaction. Joseph was a tall fourteen-year-old, thin as a beanpole. Hearing Tamu's question, Joseph continued polishing his shells. As he worked, Joseph replied with disdain, "We all know what you are going to say, Tamu. It doesn't make anyone laugh, you idiot!"

"It's because Joseph was raised on the trunk of a palm tree," continued Tamu all the same. "When he finally left home, the bark stayed attached to his calves!"

Everyone laughed except Joseph, who, annoyed, folded his legs underneath him. Aru looked at him with satisfaction. That should keep the conceited boy quiet for a while. Joseph was always all too ready to give his opinion even when no one asked for it.

The boys went back to polishing their own white shells, but not for long. Fatukolo, a wiry blond eleven-year-old, had a new joke in store for them.

"My mother told me that old Thomas wants two tafuliae for giving permission to marry his daughter Mareena," he said. "And she is really ugly. You'd have to pay *me* to marry her!"

"She has the head of a dragon on a frog's body!" added Ratu as the boys as laughed.

Aru chuckled along with his friends. These five boys had been best friends for a long time. They had been inseparable since the days they had learned to walk. They all had blond hair, except for Joseph, but they still accepted him because he could find birds better than anyone.

The five boys had even created their own secret society. The group was always ready to play new tricks, and all the villagers watched out for the boys' jokes. But because the boys were lively and intelligent, they often were asked to perform important jobs around the village.

Just two days ago, for example, the chief had asked them to prepare the shells used as the traditional currency—the kastom mani (from the English "custom money"). This job, which the boys were now performing, required patience and precision. Small white shells (collected from the sea by the men of the village) were polished on a long piece of wood. Each shell first had to be carefully cleaned and its edges scraped. Next each shell was polished and strung with the others on a cord.

After the boys had finished one set of shells, they knotted the two ends of the cord and placed it behind them. A man then picked it up and took it to a group of women who sat off to the side, near the hut of the ancestors. The women then continued the task of preparing the shells.

A humming, like the sound of a swarm of bees, rose from the group of women. They worked in teams—some drilled holes in the shells, others polished the edges to make them even, while still others placed the shells in the fire. Depending on the amount of time they were left in the fire, the shells turned a color that ranged from brown to ocher. Each shade corresponded to a certain value—the dark shells were worth more than light ones.

The last group of workers, which consisted of the oldest women in the village, sorted the shells according to color, then slipped them onto long, fibrous cords of up to 23 feet (7 meters) long.

When four of the "money belts" were ready, two men sitting in the shade of a palm tree were called over. They gently picked up the tafuliae and placed them in the ancestors' hut. The precious kastom mani was to remain in the magic darkness for about a week, the time necessary for the spirits to accept the money and grant it their blessing.

Aru and his friends knew that other kinds of money existed and were used throughout the islands, even on Malaita. This currency, made of paper or metal, was the white people's money. It had a strange name.

"Say, Tamu, what is the white man's money called?" asked Aru. "The one used to pay for things in Honiara, you know? Dowar or dovar, I can't remember."

"Dolbar," answered Tamu knowingly. "They use dolbars."

"No," interrupted Joseph with a smug look. "They're called dollars."

Aru was forced to admit that Joseph was right once again. That was the name of the money. But how could those strips of paper and pieces of metal ever replace the precious kastom mani of the ancestors?

The young boy sighed. Somewhere deep inside, a small voice told him that one day, even he would have to use the white people's money. Because, eventually, there would be no other kind of currency.

"Papa, today I fought with Tamu," said Aru. "He is furious with me because I was chosen for the path of Great Knowledge and he wasn't."

"What does it matter? You were chosen. The Council of Elders decided."

"But Tamu says that his hair is lighter than mine and that he deserves to be the son of the shark more than I do."

"That's nonsense, my son, believe me," replied Ambu. "It's not enough to be blond to become an initiate. There must be many other signs."

"Like what?"

"It's very complicated. Here, for example, look under your left arm. Do you see this light mark on your skin? It's one of the signs we recognized, just like the tooth-shaped mole you have just below your lip."

"Are there other signs?" asked Aru.

"Many others. And that's why the Council of Elders declared that the spirit of Akua, the ancestor of our clan, lives within you. Do you remember? I told you about it."

"Yes, Papa, I remember that Akua was a direct descendant of the shark-god. But I have trouble understanding that story. Can you tell it to me again? We have time today."

Seated before a fire in the dark hut, Ambu repeated the legend of the Kwara'ae to his son.

"Long, long ago, long before our fathers and grandfathers, the world—as we know it today—didn't exist. There was no sky, no sea, no earth.

"One day, what was above and what was below appeared together at the same time. First the earth rose up, flat and sterile. Then the ocean—with no tides or waves—encircled the land and pushed it so hard that the mountains and valleys were created.

"Much later, the first Basana (Creator Spirit) lived in our world. He had long black hair. He created the trees, pigs, plants, and fish. Then, because he was bored, he sculpted three wooden statues. He brought them to life by blowing on them.

"This was the creation of the Great Man of the Earth, the Great Man of the Forest, and the Great Man of the Sea. The first man planted taro, the second hunted animals, and the third was a fisherman. And then, because they grew bored, the men asked Basana to make companions for them. In this way, each of them received a woman, and the three couples lived happily for a time and produced many children.

"But one day, Basana's twin brother appeared. He was jealous and wanted to destroy his brother's work. He sent death, illness, and typhoons to strike the Great Men and their families. But Basana protected them.

"So the evil spirit brother took hold of the men's hearts instead and gave them doubt and ingratitude. But his spells didn't work on one of them—the Great Man of the Sea. The other two men no longer honored their creator and finally forgot all about him. The Great Man of the Sea never stopped talking of Basana to his two brothers, trying to get them to return to reason. The others, tired of his reproaches, decided to get rid of him. One night, they knocked him out, threw him in a dugout canoe, and pushed him toward the open sea. And that was the last anyone ever heard of him.

"Until the day when an unknown illness struck the country. The Great Men, who had forgotten their creator, no longer knew whom to ask for help. They wandered around the forest, moaning and crying. Their sons died in front of their eyes.

"One of the men was so desperate that he tried to drown himself in the sea. But just as he was about to sink under the waves, an extremely powerful being raised him to the surface. It was an enormous white shark that returned the man to shore.

"The shark spoke to the man: 'In the form in which you now see me, I hold the spirit of the only upright man this country has ever known, the Great Man of the Sea. Return to your family and tell them to rediscover the voice of Basana. I will help you by sending children with blond hair who will become medicine men. They will be my sons and will guide you. You will know them from other children by their fair hair. I will accept food from these children only.'

"Thus spoke the great shark before he swam away. Since that day, the descendants of the Great Men have always tried to follow this commandment."

Ambu stopped speaking and watched the dancing fire. A great silence came over the hut. Aru, his eyes shining, asked, "So I am a son of the shark, Papa?"

"That is what the Council said."

"But you, Papa, what do you think?"

"I think you are different from the others, my son. I sense unknown powers in you. I am very proud that you were born into my family."

"But are you my real father, Papa?"

"Yes, of course, Aru. But you have more than my blood. You contain the spirit of the clan, and you carry the line of the Great Man of the Sea."

Aru, suddenly aware of the importance of his destiny, snuggled tightly into his father's arms. He was proud to be one of the chosen, but this was a heavy burden for a twelve-year-old boy.

The spray whipped Aru's face. Perched on the tip of the dugout canoe, he watched the tapered bow plough through the silvery waves. The sun was just coming up, and the ocean was turning blue-green. A dozen boats, each filled with four or five men, followed Aru's canoe.

They had all left before dawn, as it was an important day—the previous day, fishermen had spotted huge schools of bonitos (striped-back tuna). If the fishing was good, the entire village would have enough to eat for a long time. That was why each year everyone anxiously awaited the sacred day when the fish reached Malaita.

In the stern of his canoe, Joseph waved his arms wildly. "Look! Over there! The birds!" Birds circling above the sea were the surest way to find the bonitos. The seabirds fed on the countless small fish that followed the schools.

The canoes immediately veered off. In a few minutes, they had all reached the area marked by the birds. There they could see the thousands of fish that swarmed under the water. It was a spectacular sight. All around the canoes, the sea bubbled with the confused movements of the fish that dove and returned to the surface, sharpening the appetites of the seabirds.

Aru jumped and squirmed with impatience, almost tipping his canoe. He watched as nets and harpoons flew from the fishermen's hands and landed in the blood-stained water. Although blood could attract sharks, two fishermen jumped into the water to pull in the nets. The silver bonitos were soon piled high in the bottom of the canoes, and the fishermen sang at the top of their voices.

In a nearby boat, Tamu was jumping up and down, while Fatukolo let out shrieks of excitement. Aru leaned over from his own canoe and grabbed the fish offered by the ocean with his bare hands, letting them slither down the length of his body. What a day of fishing!

One of the fishermen fell to his knees in his canoe and yelled, "Thanks to the shark!"

"Thanks be to Basana!" cried another.

Everyone rejoiced. The men sang, yelled, and cried.

"Son of the shark, you have brought us good luck!" declared a voice in the crowd. "Glory be to you, your father, and your ancestors!"

Aru, with tears in his eyes, looked around at all the joyful and thankful faces turned toward him. His throat tightened—never before had he experienced such intense emotion. A wave higher than the others splashed him, and the saltwater running down his face mixed with tears he could no longer hold back.

His father and the Council of Elders had not been wrong in recognizing a mysterious power in the boy. Aru now knew it to be true and realized he must now learn to control his power. But Aru also knew he would grow wiser with each passing day. His future was to become a great priest, and he no longer doubted himself. Overwhelmed by a great happiness, Aru knew in his heart that he really was the son of the shark.

Pictures

The Solomon Islands are a vast and varied archipelago, covered with luxurious tropical vegetation. The islands are home to a large number of ethnic groups who have preserved many of their ancestral traditions.

The people of Melanesia live in close contact with nature. The forest provides them with much of what they need to live, including wood and palm leaves.

Melanesians use natural fibers, flowers,

The Kwara'ae believe that blond children

shells, and feathers to make jewelry.

are descended from the great white shark.

Aru heads into the forest to collect medicinal plants. He keeps an eye out for dangerous animals and members of enemy tribes.

Malaita is the most traditional of the Solomon Islands. Initiation rituals, magic ceremonies, ancestor worship, and other traditions have been carefully protected from outside influence. Life on the island has continued in much the same way for centuries.

The rituals of daily life in the Solomon Islands have not changed for centuries. But many islanders worry about the future and wonder if their traditions will continue to survive.

Notebook

Geography

The Solomon Islands are located in the western Pacific Ocean, at 159° **longitude** east and 8° **latitude** south—virtually on the equator. The country consists of six main islands (Guadalcanal, New Georgia, San Cristobal, Malaita, Santa Isabel, and Choiseul), 30 smaller islands, and about 950 **atolls.** With 370,000 total inhabitants, the island group is the most populated archipelago in the Pacific Ocean. The Solomon Islands are part of the Pacific Ring of Fire, a circle in the Pacific Ocean rimmed with volcanic islands and mountains. Located on a crack in the earth's crust, the islands on the Ring of Fire often experience earthquakes and volcanic activity. In 1981, a record-breaking year, 1,908 earthquakes were registered in the Solomon Islands. The island of Malaita has a surface area of 1,870 square miles (4,843 square kilometers). About 97,000 people live on Malaita, making it the most populated island in the Solomons.

CHINA
Hanoi
LAOS
VIETNAM
THAILAND
Bangkok
CAMBODIA
Pnompenh
Ho Chi Minh City
South China Sea
Manila
Mindan
MALAYSIA
Kuala Lumpur
Singapore
Celebes S
Borneo
Celeb
Sumatra
Java Sea
Djakarta
INDONESI
Java

INDIAN OCEAN

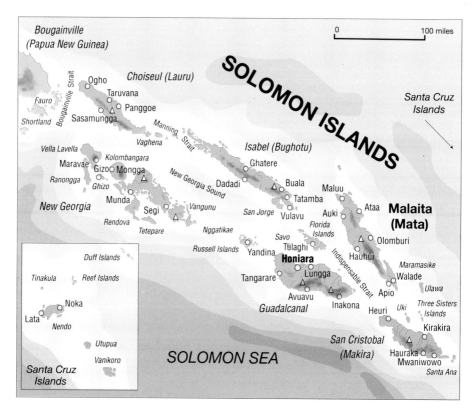

Malaita

The name of the island, which is pronounced mah-LAY-tah, is the latest in a long series of names. When Spanish explorer Alvaro de Mendana first spotted the island in the 1500s, he named it Ramos, the Spanish word for tree branches. In 1767 English explorer Philip Carteret renamed the island after himself. Later, it became Malayette or Malanta. The local tribes often called it Mata.

Official name: Solomon Islands
Capital: Honiara
Surface area:
11,500 square miles
(29,783 square kilometers)
Population: 368,000
Official currency:
Solomon Islands dollar
Languages: English and
Melanesian dialects

40

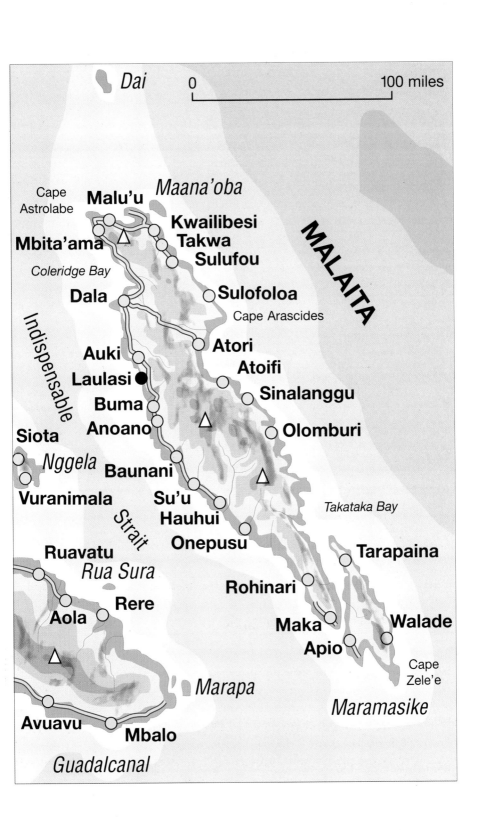

Dai

0   100 miles

Maana'oba

MALAITA

Cape
Astrolabe

Malu'u

Kwailibesi
Takwa
Sulufou

Mbita'ama

Coleridge Bay

Dala

Sulofoloa

Cape Arascides

Indispensable

Auki

Atori
Atoifi

Laulasi ●

Buma

Sinalanggu

Anoano

Siota

Olomburi

Nggela **Baunani**

Vuranimala

Su'u
Hauhui

Onepusu

Takataka Bay

Strait

Ruavatu
Rua Sura

Tarapaina

Rere

Rohinari

Aola

Maka

Walade

Apio

Cape
Zele'e

Marapa

Maramasike

Avuavu

Mbalo

Guadalcanal

A Hot and Humid Climate

The Solomon Islands consist of two long rows of mountainous islands. The highest mountain in the archipelago is Makarakombu, on Guadalcanal Island. This peak rises 8,028 feet (2,447 meters). The natural mountain barrier blocks the path of passing clouds, causing them to drop heavy rainfall on the hillsides and even more in the lowlands.

The Solomon Islands have a **tropical** climate. The heavy rains of the monsoons accentuate the wet, steamy weather— especially on the southern islands. The average annual rainfall exceeds 120 inches (305 centimeters) and can even reach 500 inches

The mountains are covered with thick tropical vegetation.

(1,270 cm) along the southern coast of Guadalcanal. The average temperature ranges from 70° F to 90° F (21° to 32° C). The hot, wet climate has encouraged the growth of the thick forests that cover all the islands.

Palm tree and mangrove tree

An Exposed Archipelago

Cyclones are common in the Solomon Islands. These windstorms occur mainly between January and April, frequently resulting in deaths and destruction of property.

The island paradise can be upset by cyclones.

A Fortress Island

The inhabitants of Malaita say their island is shaped like a sleeping dog on its haunches. From a boat off the coast, the island looks like a fortress. Rough coastlines makes it difficult to reach the island from the sea. The deep waters of the Indispensable Strait isolate Malaita from the archipelago's other large islands.

Inland areas on the island are also extremely difficult to penetrate. The central mountains are surrounded by high, rugged plateaus. Thick tropical vegetation covers the island.

The Artificial Islands

Malaita is surrounded by artificial islands. The largest artificial island measures 46 square miles (119 sq km). These small islands were constructed by the native population so that people could flee to safer ground when conflicts occurred on

Shark and dolphin

Malaita. Over time, residents have piled rocks and stones on

sandbars and coral reefs. Aru's family lives on the artificial island of Laulasi. Traditionally, young couples construct their own islands, creating enough space for

their descendants and their allies.

Crocodile

Key Facts

- The climate of the Solomon Islands is tropical.
- Cyclones strike the islands frequently, especially from January to April.
- The island of Malaita is surrounded by small artificial islands.

43

People and Their Work

Diverse groups of people live on the islands of Melanesia. From left to right: a boy from Bougainville—an island in the country of Papua New Guinea—has dark features. A Solomon Islander has light hair. A woman from Fiji, a group of islands southeast of the Solomons, has light-brown skin and dark, tightly curled hair.

The Melanesian Population

The population of the Pacific Ocean can be divided into three main groups. In the east and the center live the Polynesians, in the northwest reside the Micronesians, and in the southwest are the Melanesians. The Polynesians and the Micronesians share physical traits, such as copper-colored skin. Melanesians have dark skin, and their faces are shaped differently.

Geographically, Melanesia includes Papua New Guinea, the Solomon Islands, Vanuatu, New Caledonia, and the Fiji Islands. Melanesia consists of some 30 main islands, 300 small islands, and thousands of atolls.

A Melanesian.

Five and a half million people live in Melanesia. The population of Malaita is different from that of other islands. Thirteen distinct ethnic groups share this land. Until the 1920s, cannibalism and headhunting were common on the island. No one from the outside could conquer the island's ferocious warriors. Each ethnic group still claims its own territory and has its own customs. Violent conflicts still sometimes erupt between some of these groups.

44

Malaita

The small island of Maana'omba off Malaita's northeast coast, the nearby artificial islands of the Lau Lagoon, and Fanafei Island in the southeast are inhabited by the Lau tribe. The island of Maramasike in the southeast is shared by people known as the Are Are and the Saa. Most of Malaita's inhabitants are subsistence farmers or fishers.

The Blond Children of Malaita

Fair-haired people usually have low levels of melanin, the pigment that also gives skin its color. On Malaita, however, even the blond children have dark skin and eyes. No one knows why these people have dark skin and such light hair. Their blond hair is lightened even more because they bleach it with lime.

One of the many theories claims that this fair hair dates from contact with white people many years ago. Yet no white-skinned people met the inhabitants of the Solomon Islands until the 1500s. Furthermore, the first Spanish explorers to reach the Solomon Islands took note of the blond-haired children.

Fishing

Since the 1970s, fishing—the traditional work of the archipelago's population—has become one of the main sources of income for the Solomon Islands. This is mainly due to the development of small fishing industries on a few of the larger islands. Exports of fish—mainly tuna—earn a significant amount of money.

In 1978 the country created an exclusive fishing area extending 200 miles (322 km) out from its coastlines to protect local fishers. Problems immediately arose when larger nations, including the former Soviet Union and the United States, set up a blockade around the Solomon Islands. This action forced the nation to accept the presence of large, modern fishing fleets, including a number of giant Japanese fishing boats and new processing plants. The arrival of the Japanese and their fishing techniques, particularly the use of drift nets that quickly depopulate the seabed, severely damaged the local fishing industry.

Net fishing is common in the waters around Laulasi.

Forestry

Forests cover almost all of the islands in the archipelago. Logging companies, most of which are foreign owned, harvest about 10 percent of the available wood each year. Most of the lumber is exported to Japan. But the forest industry has slowed down in recent years because of protests from the clans. These groups own the land and object to the destruction of their ancestral home. Plans have been made to replace the trees that were cut down haphazardly.

Key Facts
- Fishing represents an important source of income for the Solomon Islanders.
- The archipelago also earns money from copra, almonds, cacao, and coconuts.

46

Agriculture

About 80 percent of Solomon Islanders farm for a living. Yet agricultural techniques on the Solomon Islands are underdeveloped. Everyone grows just enough food for their own needs. Until the 1980s, the coconut palm, which produces copra, provided most of the income. Since then, the price of coconut oil has fallen because other oils made from artificial ingredients cost less. New crops—such as rice, cacao, and spices—are also being grown.

This farmer is carrying a yam, a basic food in the Melanesian diet.

Fishers sell bonitos on the beach at Auki, the capital of the island of Malaita.

Copra

Copra is the dried meat of a shelled coconut, which is then pressed for its oil. The name copra comes from Tamil (the language of southern India). The coconut consists of a thick, fibrous external shell that surrounds the thinner inside shell. This inner shell protects a white layer of meat and the coconut milk in the center. The

dried meat, or copra, is 65 percent oil. This oil is used to make cooking oil, margarine, and cosmetics. Much of the income of the Solomon Islands comes from the copra industry.

47

History

A Long History of Violence

The first Melanesians are thought to have arrived in the Solomon archipelago around 4,000 years ago. At first, the people hunted and gathered their food. They later adopted farming, which allowed them to settle permanently on the land. Between 1200 and 1600 A.D., small groups of Polynesians from the east reached the eastern Solomon Islands. The early contacts between Polynesians and Melanesians were peaceful, but the two groups later became enemies. From the fourteenth to the seventeenth centuries, the islanders were victims of raids by the Tongans, who came from an island group southeast of the Solomon Islands.

Highly decorated warriors fought in battles between the various tribes and against European newcomers.

48

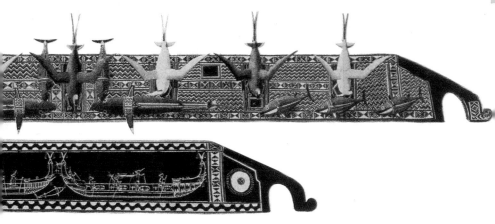

Mendana's Expeditions

In 1567, a Spanish expedition led by Don Alvaro de Mendana Neira, nephew of the viceroy (ruler) of Peru, left South America in two ships. Its mission was to discover "the great islands to the west," which Mendana and his sailors believed were Ophir and Tarsis—the islands of the legendary mines of King Solomon, an ancient ruler of Israel.

After two difficult months at sea, the crews discovered and explored an unknown archipelago. Four months later, the exhausted sailors returned to Peru. Mendana, thinking that he had in fact discovered the islands of King Solomon, named them after the monarch.

Mendana was convinced the Solomon archipelago contained untold wealth. For 27 years, he repeatedly asked the king of Spain to fund a new expedition. In 1595, Mendana finally set sail again with 4 ships and 400 sailors, most of whom brought along their families. Mendana's own wife, Dona Isabela, also came along. The group's mission was to found a new colony in the Solomons.

Mendana was never able to find the same islands again.

The dugout canoe has existed as a means of transportation for thousands of years.

He reached an unknown island that he named Santa Cruz (now called Ndeni, the name given to the island by the native people). The islanders and the Spaniards distrusted one another, and the conflicts that followed finally convinced the colonists to leave.

49

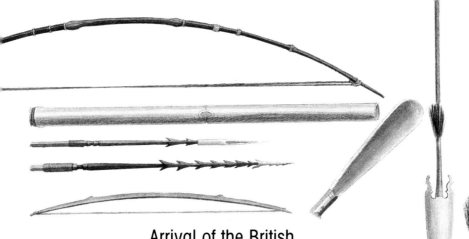

Arrival of the British

In 1767, British explorer Philip Carteret landed on Malaita. From that time on, large numbers of Europeans traveled to the archipelago. As their numbers increased, the newcomers saw their shaky peace with the natives deteriorate.

Conflicts erupted, caused mainly by the Europeans' desire to take anything of value. Europeans also tried to force the Christian religion on the islanders, who had their own form of worship. In addition, thousands of islanders died from diseases carried by the colonists.

For these reasons, the islanders attacked the colonists. The archipelago quickly acquired the reputation of being the most dangerous area in the Pacific. The British responded by raiding native villages. Later, the British kidnapped residents to work on faraway plantations. By the end of the 1800s, the archipelago officially became a British protectorate.

Encounters between European explorers and the islanders were often hostile.

50

The Rise of Nationalism

The native peoples rebelled against the British. By the mid-1900s, organized groups were calling for independence. In 1970 the British agreed to allow an elected government council. Independence was finally granted to the Solomon Islands in 1978.

Key Facts

- The first inhabitants reached the archipelago approximately 4,000 years ago.
- The Spanish sailor Alvaro de Mendana explored the archipelago in 1567.

Malaita

The island remained for the most part sheltered from European expeditions until the nineteenth century. In 1829, a European whaling boat was shipwrecked off the coast. Twenty sailors managed to reach land and were eaten by cannibals. Later, the arrival of missionaries—who came to establish the Christian religion among the islanders—only worsened the tension.

Independence

Malaitans have always wanted to remain independent from any outside rule. They revolted against colonizers many times. In 1927, for example, the Kwaio mounted an attack on British authorities trying to collect taxes and confiscate weapons. An organized movement for independence began on Malaita in the mid-1900s. Even today, many people on Malaita refuse to recognize the authority of the central government in Honiara and still demand full independence.

Cultural Life

Importance of Tradition

Traditions on Malaita have outlived many of those of the other islands. One example of Malaita's unique character is tribal warfare. Tribal conflicts have died down or are at least rare throughout most of the Solomon Islands. On Malaita, however, clan rivalry often still turns into ethnic warfare.

Cults devoted to spirits, the worship of ancestors, and the practice of shamanism and witchcraft still continue on Malaita. All these beliefs and practices, attacked on the Solomon Islands by Christian missionaries and authorities in Honiara, remain very active on Malaita. Some of these traditions are even gaining ground that had been lost in the early 1900s during the most active period of the Christian missionaries.

The Kwara'ae craft their own fishing gear, including canoe paddles (above) and fishing nets (left). By carrying on traditions such as these, the Kwara'ae avoid depending on outsiders for the goods they need.

52

Customs on the Solomon Islands

Melanesia, the most populated region of the Pacific, has the richest and most diverse culture. Thousands of languages, art forms, religions, and traditions exist here. The Solomon Islands play an important role in the region. Here are some of the special customs of this country.

The Cult of the Shark

The mystery and dangers of the sea have inspired many legends and beliefs among the inhabitants of the Solomon Islands. Sharks have been both feared and revered for centuries. Numerous cults worship the shark to obtain its protection and calm its anger. One of these cults is in the village of Laulasi.

The people of Laulasi believe that the spirits of their ancestors come back to life as sharks. During ceremonies, young male initiates offer the fresh meat of sacrificed animals to the sharks. Enormous sharks seize the food from the hands of the boys without attacking them. Occasionally, a boy who is in a trance will grasp a shark's fin and be pulled a short distance.

Dances, statues, and other forms of art honor the shark-god.

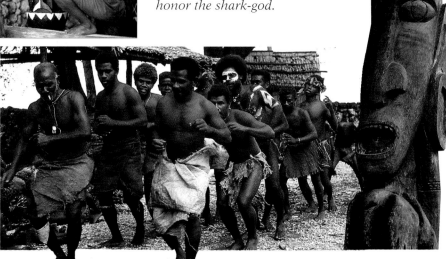

53

A Land-based Culture

Many inhabitants of Malaita are known as the mountain people of the sea. About 16,000 Malaitans have no contact whatsoever with the ocean, which they consider to be inhabited by demons. Even some islanders who live close to the coast do not make use of the ocean. The lifestyle of these inland people is traditionally more conservative than the casual lifestyle of fishers and sailors.

Feathers and Shells as Currency

In addition to the official currency—the Solomon Islands dollar—several other types of kastom mani (custom money) exist. These are the only currencies accepted for the purchase of land, payment of damages, and agreements of marriage.

A wife is purchased by offering the bride's father a high payment. Some young men put themselves and their families into debt to obtain the amount demanded. This sum is not measured in dollars, but in kastom mani. The most valuable of these currencies are rolls of red feathers from Ndeni (these rolls may be up to 33 feet/10 m long), the kesa from Choiseul (made with 9 rare, large cylindrical shells), and the tafuliae from Malaita (large strips made up of 10 rows of small disks sculpted from shells and strung on cords).

This young man is polishing shells that will be threaded onto long strings to make tafuliae.

54

The Wantok

The pidgin term "wantok" (from "one talk") refers to everyone who speaks a single language. In the traditional society of the Solomon Islands, wantok defines relationships between individuals. Wantok has created a social system in which people who speak a single language help one another and feel a sense of kinship. Members of the same family are wantoks—so are neighbors and all the people in the village, the clan, and the tribe who speak the same dialect.

During local festivals, children gather in the home of the elders and participate in games.

Pidgin and Kastom

Pidgin is a dialect used in the Papuan and Melanesian regions. Using pidgin, many small local tribes that speak different languages can understand one another. Pidgin is based on English, Chinese, Indonesian, Papuan, and Melanesian words.

Kastom is the pidgin word that corresponds to the English word "custom." Kastom determines every moment of daily life for the islanders. It defines everything— from a decision about where to build a new home to the style of clothes worn and the manner of honoring ancestors. Kastom governs invisible spirits, magic, and the afterworld. Despite governmental efforts to reduce its influence, kastom remains a recognized form of law among the inhabitants of the archipelago.

The Shaman

The system of **taboos** is governed by strict laws and is passed on by traditional shamans, who are priests and healers. Shamans are believed to have the power to contact ancestors and the spirits of the forest or water. Shamans use magic and witchcraft, and the secrets of these arts, which are carefully guarded, are usually handed down from father to son. The priests practice techniques of natural medicine and are said to cast evil spells on their enemies.

For more than two centuries, shamans have been the target of the missionaries, many of whom tried to destroy everything they considered to be pagan (without religion). This intolerance led to the demise of many cults, art forms, dances, and oral traditions. But because kastom has resisted this influence, important aspects of the past remain and often have been integrated into the Christian religion.

Officially, 85 percent of Solomon Is-

This Kwara'ae priest knows the secrets of the shark cult.

landers are Christians, although many of these people also practice their traditional religions. Yet the old religions are growing stronger as Christianity, which did not deliver a promise of paradise to the native people, loses its influence.

The warriors also respect kastom.

56

The Cargo Cult

This cult, which affected a large part of Melanesia, appeared with the arrival of U.S. soldiers during World War II. The Melanesians were struck by the vast quantity of food, clothing, and equipment brought as cargo by the North Americans. The islanders believed that if they adopted the Christian faith, a cargo god would provide them with all the goods they needed.

The islanders asked the Christian missionaries to help them adopt this new religion, and the cargo cult was born. The missionaries, pleased that they could finally convert the island's inhabitants, did not attempt to explain what a ship and its cargo really were. The cargo cult has nearly died out.

Taboo

Taboo designates both sacred and forbidden actions. Breaking a taboo is a serious matter and is believed to anger the spirits.

A woman who enters a certain temple, a person who steps over someone who is seated or sleeping, or a man who walks under drying laundry are all considered to be breaking a taboo. Depending on the gravity of the offense, failure to respect a taboo can result in a simple fine or may involve banishment from the village. In early years, breaking a taboo could mean death for the offender

The skulls of ancestors are believed to protect the village. They are kept in special enclosures.

Glossary

archipelago (ahr-kuh-PEH-luh-goh) A cluster of islands in a large body of water. Many archipelagoes are made up of volcanic islands, a large number of which are located in the Pacific Ocean.

atoll (A-tawl) A ring-shaped coral reef that surrounds a shallow body of water called a lagoon. Atolls, most of which are found in the Pacific Ocean, are formed on sunken banks of land or on the rims of sunken volcanoes.

dysentery (DIH-suhn-tehr-ee) A disease of the intestines caused by infection.

latitude The distance, measured in degrees, to the north or south of the equator—an imaginary line on maps and globes that circles the middle of the earth.

longitude The distance measured in degrees, to the east or west of the prime meridian—an imaginary line on maps and globes that runs north to south through Greenwich, England.

medicine man A person with spiritual powers who treats the sick and injured. A medicine man is also known as a healer or shaman.

taboo A rule forbidding certain actions or practices.

tropic An area on either side of the equator where the climate is hot and humid.

Index

Acknowledgments

All photos by Alain Chenevière except the following: Musée national d'histoire naturelle (France), pp. 37, 48–49, 50–51; Artwork by Anne Bodin, pp. 4–24, 37, 42, 43, 47; Maps by Patrick Mérienne, pp. 39, 40, 41